A PILLOW BOOK

SUZANNE BUFFAM

CANARIUM BOOKS
ANN ARBOR, MARFA, IOWA CITY

SPONSORED BY
THE HELEN ZELL WRITERS' PROGRAM
AT THE UNIVERSITY OF MICHIGAN

A PILLOW BOOK

Canarium Books
Ann Arbor, Marfa, Iowa City
www.canarium.org

The editors gratefully acknowledge the
Helen Zell Writers' Program at the University of Michigan
for editorial assistance and generous support.

Cover design: Alysia Shewchuk
Cover image: © Shutterstock
Cover reproduced with permission
of House of Anansi Press.

Author portrait: © Mira Buffam Reddy
Used with permission of the artist.

First Edition
Third Printing

Printed in the United States of America

ISBN 13: 978-0-9969827-0-2

for my mother

A PILLOW BOOK

Among the oldest living pillows in the world today is a smooth block of unpainted wood with a wide crack running through its middle and a shallow indentation on the top. It was found in the tomb of an Egyptian mummy in the Fourth Dynastic town of Gebelein, on the banks of the Nile River. If you came across it in a field, you might assume it had just fallen from a cart. If you found it by the sea, you might suppose it had been knocked loose from a sailboat in a storm. You might kick it, or pick it up and toss it like a bottle off the dock.

●

F. Scott Fitzgerald wrote lists. Abraham Lincoln took midnight walks. Tallulah Bankhead paid a series of young caddies to hold her hand in the dark, as did Marcel Proust. Thomas Edison invented the light bulb so he could read after dark. I put a piece of paper under my pillow at night, and when I could not sleep, I wrote in the dark, wrote Henry David Thoreau, who once spent a fortnight in a roofless cabin with his head on a pillow of bricks.

●

There are two kinds of insomniacs: those who fall asleep easily, only to wake up hours later to toss on their pillows until dawn; and those who toss on their pillows from the start, only to drift off just long enough to be roused at dawn by the crows. A little game I like to play, when I crawl into bed at the end of a long day of anything, these days, is to guess which kind, tonight, I will be.

●

BOOKS I'D LIKE TO READ SOMEDAY

I and It, by Martin Buber.
Queen Lear, by William Shakespeare.
Moby Dick, by Gertrude Stein.

End Game, by Dr. Seuss.
Complete Poems, by Sappho.
The Interpretation of Dreams, by Jorge Luis Borges.
Kafka for Dummies, by Franz Kafka.
My Mistake, by Laura Bush.
What Would Jesus Do?, by Jesus Christ.

●

Sei Shōnagon's *Pillow Book*, which has passed the last several nights in the dim glow of my Petzel Tikinna 2 headlamp set on low, provides an exhaustive catalogue of petty grievances, as pressing today as they were a millennium ago. One has gone to bed and is about to doze off, the Lady complains in her protracted list of Hateful Things, when a mosquito appears, announcing himself in a reedy voice. One can actually feel the wind made by his wings and, slight though it is, one finds it hateful in the extreme. I would add to this list—as I often feel it incumbent upon me to do—the endless, intermittent tinkling, through the half-open window screen, of one's deaf neighbor's wind chimes; the pre-dawn, post-amorous blather of young robins from the treetops; and one's husband squinting peevishly from his pillow at night when one turns on the bathroom light to fish one's dripping headlamp from the toilet bowl.

◐

Kings and commoners alike have known the value of a good pillow forever. From Quito to Cairo to Chicago to Xiangyang, examples can be found in museums all over the world. During my sleepless hours some nights I try to imagine the whole collection.

◐

Melatonin. Lunesta. Nyquil. Zzzquil. Ativan. Ambien. Lorazepam. Trazodone. Warm milk. Hot baths. Counting sheep. Counting backwards from a thousand in French. Still I toss and turn through the night with a pillow on my head and another clutched like a mule between my knees.

◐

Some nights I search for solutions online. On Google Shopping I find the Sobakawa Cloud, as seen on TV, with over thirty million cooling micro-air beads to conform to my shoulders and neck, while cradling my head in a fluffy cloud of nanotechnology. A pillow over three hundred years in the making, based on traditional Japanese buckwheat hull pillows, it can be mine for only $19.99. The promotional video, with its barbells and broken eggshells, is persuasive. Off-putting, however, is the manufacturer's subtle but emphatic prohibition against removing or in any way washing its custom-fit pillowcase, which must be ordered separately at an additional charge.

○

The world has been a trifle 'slow' on the subject of pillows, notes a column in the October 1894 issue of *The Decorator and Furnisher* magazine, advertising, in lieu of feathers or fiber, a row of sturdy steel springs wrapped in cotton batting and stitched up inside a stiff cotton sack. Air is the principal thing, the faded copy insists. Plenty of pure, life-giving oxygen, freely inhaled in the silent watches of the night, gives the crown of beauty to the woman, mental vigor to the man, and the halo of promise to the little folk. Not surprisingly, alas, according to Volume One of *Obsolete American Securities and Corporations*, the Columbus Spring Pillow Company, along with its ill-fated "pillow with lungs," exhaled its dying breath into the night above New Jersey in 1896.

○

Later that fall in West Orange, New Jersey, Thomas Edison staged the first pillow fight ever recorded on film. From Edison's catalogue: four young ladies, in their nightgowns, having a romp. One of the pillows gets torn, and the feathers fly all over the room. 45 feet. $6.75.

O

DREAM JOBS

Random Link Clicker.
Royal Bath Taker.
Receiver of Foot Rubs and Praise.
Chief Executive Napper.
Undersecretary of Trivial Pursuits.
Jester to Her Empirical Majesty of Unverifiable Facts.
Procurer of Unnecessary Hats.
Empress of Ice Cream.
Cloud-Development Supervisor.
Inspector General of Minor Slights.
Editorial Dictator-in-Residence.
Bubble Blower to the Stars.

O

Sei was her father's name, Shōnagon her father's rank. For a brief span of time at the turn of the tenth century, we know that she spent her nights behind a thin paper screen, recording her fugitive aperçus by candlelight with an ink stick on rice paper behind the bolted Heian gates. We know that she slept, when she managed to do so, on a small, hollow pillow made of polished bamboo.

○

Things to buy. Things to fix. Things to fold. Things to freeze. Things to paint. Things to unpack. Things to order. Things to renew. Things to revise. Things to discard. Things to dismantle. Things to destroy. The closest I come to writing poems these days are the lists I jot down in the little blue notebook I keep beside my pillow to remind myself, years hence, how my middle years were spent.

○

UNMARKED DAYS

Belabor Day.
World Day Against the Abuse of Perfume.
World Back Talk Prevention Day.
International Day for the Complete Eradication of Goatees.
International Day for the Right to the Truth Concerning Hidden
    Calories in Juice.
United Nations International Day in Support of the Victims of
    Screen Fatigue.
International Day in Remembrance of Diaries Altered and
    Burned.
Day of the Sleepwalker.
Day of the Streetwalker.
International Day of the Overripe Pear.
Daylight Spendings Day.

Divorcee Day.

World Day for the Promulgation and Diffusion of Fog.

Anti-Dabbler Day.

Doris Day Day.

World Day for the Remembrance of the Tiny Hands of the
Tyrannosaurus Rex.

○

I can swim, Her Majesty proclaims from her pillow one morning.
By this she means that she can cling to my neck in the shallow end
of the university pool while I clap and sing a bouncy song about
rain to the tune of "I'm a Little Teapot" with a flagging chorus of
other mothers. In the locker room, the toddlers shriek and squirm
in sagging swim diapers while we womenfolk sigh and hide behind
our towels. Bolted to the ceiling in the corner above the sinks,
the TV, perpetually tuned to CNN, crackles with the constant
chatter of catastrophe unfolding on the far side of the screen. Her
Majesty, I am grateful to observe, has not yet spotted it.

○

Nightsweats? Hot flashes? Headaches? Fever? Migraines? Insect
bites? Sore, tired feet? Turn your pillow into a Chillow, for
only $12.95, using a patented, eco-friendly, hypo-allergenic,
latex-free, phlalate-free, gel-free, battery-free, medical-grade
foam insert, available exclusively online, and activated instantly

when filled with four pints of ordinary tap water. The hour-long promotional program on Ideal World Channel features the company's affable British CEO fielding scripted questions from a chatty and conspicuously well-rested looking host. The five hundred and seven customer reviews to date on Amazon.com, it bears noting, average only three-and-a-half stars out of five. Would not recommend to anyone except my former mother-in-law, reports Redhead3970, whose bright white patented Comfort Device sprung a fatal leak within two weeks, and whose comments are typed in all caps.

O

BAD IDEAS THAT WOULD PROBABLY SELL

Camouflage diapers.
Hummingbird cacciatore.
Hamster camp.
Stationary tricycles.
Diet ice.

O

My husband can sleep anywhere. I have a traveling exhibit's worth of shots of him sprawled with his hands behind his head and a beatific grin across his face while my twisted shadow darkens the flimsy excuse for a pillow beside him in hostels, rustic sheds, three-star hotels, and stuffy guest suites across North America, continental Europe, and far-flung regions of Southeast Asia. Do opposites attract? Unresolved patterns attract, avers Paul Cutright, director of the Center for Enlightened Partnerships in Las Vegas and author of the best-selling *You're Never Upset for the Reason You Think*, whose flawless bridgework surfaced on my pillow at four a.m. today in a Health and Sex feature I happened across in the dark.

○

NATO INTERNATIONAL RADIOTELEPHONY CODE WORDS A TO Z

Alpha.
Bravo.
Charlie.
Delta.
Echo.
Foxtrot.
Golf.
Hotel.
India.
Juliet.
Kilo.
Lima.
Mike.
November.
Oscar.
Papa.

Quebec.
Romeo.
Sierra.
Tango.
Uniform.
Victor.
Whiskey.
X-ray.
Yankee.
Zulu.

◐

Splendid Things. Awkward Things. Things That Make One's Heart Beat Faster. Things That Give a Dirty Feeling. Things That Have Lost Their Power. Things That Should Be Small. Things That Give a Hot Feeling. Things That Cannot Be Compared. A hundred and sixty-four of Sei Shōnagon's incomparable lists have survived the tempestuous centuries. The most remarked-upon aspect of her *Pillow Book* by far, they seem to lack any literary precedent. They have been emulated, parodied, and appropriated by many, but no one knows quite what to make of them. There are *Pillow Book* scholars, I learned over crock-pot meatballs and boxed wine at a junior faculty potluck in the Quad Club last night, whose research focuses exclusively on these lists. Some are simply long catalogues of proper names—mountains, temples, islands, towns—of interest, insofar as they suggest the approximate contours of the Heian woman's world, exclusively to the scholar, allows one scholar begrudgingly.

◑

As a child I lay awake many nights on my pillow with a flashlight and a box of cards from my favorite parlor game, Trivial Pursuit. To this day, I would gladly recite which Thames bridge one must cross to get to Kew Garden; which three European countries begin with the letter A; what sport two teams of Union Army soldiers played before a crowd of 40,000 at Hilton Head, South Carolina in 1862; and what snack food a University of South Florida engineering professor spent six years studying the crunch of, if asked. I am not much fun to play with, apparently, and have gone unchallenged for years.

◑

In the quaint vernacular of chronobiology—the study of circadian rhythms' effects on the behavior, anatomy, genetics, and molecular biology of living organisms—the world is divided between owls and larks. Some people are born good sleepers and some are not. Some of us rise every morning to greet the day's labors with smiles on our dewy-fresh faces, and some of us, simply, do not. What bars owls from sleep, furthermore, is not the bungled pullout of troops from Afghanistan; not the nuclear stew off the coast of Japan; not our toddlers' pre-ballet teachers' incessant requests for Saturday morning volunteers; not the mysterious leak that sprung last month in the garage; not depression, anxiety, stress, or disrepair; but simply an inborn disposition to wander the hallways by moonlight or lie awake on one's pillow making lists.

IFFY SIMILES

Classy as a cruise ship.
Patient as a pimp.
Simple as a snowflake.
Sexy as an ankh.
Green as the Green Zone.
Cozy as a coffin.
Friendly as fire.
Easy is as easy does.

After tracing hearts with the tip of my finger across Her Majesty's back ad nauseam in the dark until losing it at last and storming off to fold socks, I step outside for a smoke under the stars. I bring my tepid Sancerre. I collapse in a wet deck chair and exhale, triggering the trigger-happy floodlight above the garage, which blinds me briefly and goes dark. For the first time all day, I'm fully awake. Snow blows in pillowy drifts along the brick wall to the west. Clouds glide overhead, downy rafts beyond reach. I pick a fixed point in the velvet abyss and make a wish: May all kamma be resolved and the mind-flower of wisdom bloom in Nibbàna's eternal spring. And may I squeeze back into last year's jeans. My star winks and turns red, and then banks to the right and heads east, in the general direction of dawn. In the distance, someone laughs, and then spits.

●

I have the sleep hygiene of a narcoleptic truck-driver on crank,
I learn on my pillow by my phone's blue glow. My failure is
moral, as much as it is physiological. Moreover, I am restless,
over-sensitive, and prone to hyperkinetic dreams, when I do
dream, that wake me sobbing in distress. I am not what is called
"a morning person," by any measure, and yet I live, alas, in a
morning person's world. If I want to get serious, as my husband
has gently suggested more than once in our marriage, I will have
to take a hard look at my habits.

●

RELUCTANT

A graduate student to graduate.
A pregnant woman to eat suckling pig.
A doctor to seek medical advice.
A CEO to pay sales tax.
Men to parallel park with their fathers-in-law in the car.
Dogs to wear fur coats.

My friend repeats a secret mantra on her pillow every night. She listens to Sigur Rós on repeat in Hopelandic while leafing through the *Harvard Medical Guide*. She swears by yoga. She swears by no screen time after six p.m.. Acupuncture, swimming, probiotics, fish oil, tart cherry extract, magnesium, iron, rowing, running, a tater tot or two before bed. She taps at her temples, chin, solar plexus, and other energy meridians, repeating that she loves and accepts herself, and that tonight she will get the good sleep she deserves. Her stepmother, a three-time widow in Vermont, now seventy-six, still beds down every night on the same trusty pillow she has slept on since she was eight. We are what we repeatedly do, was Aristotle's view of virtue.

SOONER

Sooner strangle an infant in its cradle than attend another baby shower.
Sooner starve than eat clams from a can.
Sooner join the French Foreign Legion than a book club.
Sooner sleep with a fool than wake up with a wise man.

●

If you excel at geometry, algebra, arithmetic, trigonometry, statistics, differential calculus, probabilities, or transcendental properties, you might someday tackle Charles Dodgson's knotty *Pillow Problems*, devised, he claimed, to the incredulity of many, without the aid of pen or paper, in the dark. More likely, however, you will side with the amateur Dutch mathematician, programmer, Sanskrit scholar, slap bass player, and Lewis Carroll enthusiast, J. Bogaarts, who laments in his five-star review of these problems on Amazon.com: I try to solve them when I am sleepless in bed, maybe my pillow is not right.

◐

I surface gasping on my pillow at three a.m. and turn in relief to find my husband, who has stayed up late again to watch the zombies feed on Amazon Prime, snoring soundly on his pillow beside me. I hear the soft sobbing of a siren to the south, joined by the tantrum of a fire engine's horn. I resist the urge to check the live crime feed on Facebook, but lose the rest of the night to the one hundred and one worst red carpet disasters of all time.

◐

It is so stiflingly hot in the Seventh Month that even at night one keeps all the doors and lattices open. At such times it is delightful to wake up when the moon is shining and to look outside. I enjoy it even when there is no moon. But to wake up at dawn and see a pale sliver of a moon in the sky—well, I need hardly say how perfect that is. So often does Shōnagon mention the moon it feels wrong not to read her *Pillow Book* by its blue glow. Were it not for the unrelenting slash of orange streetlight that would inundate my chamber without them, I would gladly forgo our custom-fit blackout blinds.

◗

HOME APPLIANCES A TO Z

Aeroccino machine.
Baby bullet.
Chapati maker.
Dehydrator jerky gun.
Eggstractor.
Fusion juicer.
George Foreman Grill.
High-velocity wall-mounted wind machine.
Insinkerator.
Japanese fish-shaped hot cake maker.
Kitchen anti-fatigue mat.
Laundry pod.
Magic Bullet Express Deluxe 25-piece Mixer & Blender with
    Bonus Ice Shaver Blade.
NordicTrack Incline Trainer.

One-touch automatic electric tin can opener and jar grip tool.

Personal hand-held portable battery-operated mini air fan for home or travel.

Quesadilla press.

Robotic vacuum cleaner.

Safe.

Triple tap commercial-grade built-in stainless steel outdoor kegerator deluxe.

Ultrasonic cool mist humidifier with 2.3 gallon output per day.

Vitamix.

Water pick.

Xbox.

Yard Sentinel Ultrasonic Animal Pest Bird Control Repeller with Motion Detector, Strobe & Intruder Alarm.

Zero Gravity Chaise.

◗

Recent studies link sleep, or rather the lack of it, to all manner of psycho-physiological disrepair, from high blood pressure to metabolic dysfunction, schizophrenia, and Alzheimer's, not to mention anxiety, depression, irritability, and despair. In the meltdown of Chernobyl, the leak at Three Mile Island, the Exxon Valdez oil spill, and the explosion, before a live television audience of schoolchildren across North America, of the space shuttle Challenger—to say nothing of the endless fiery stream of brisk extinctions on our freeways every day—lack of sleep played a part. Those who sleep fewer, on average, than six hours every night, live, on average, twenty percent shorter lives. Without dreams, we die quicker. No one quite knows the reason for this. We know less about what happens on our pillows at night than we know about the dark side of the moon.

◖

Her Majesty does not knock. She sits down on the mattress beside me and sighs. I am in the middle of a difficult sentence about a rare Mesopotamian pillow, made of petrified goat hair and straw, recently discovered in the rubble of a village in Iraq. I look up from my laptop and force the corners of my mouth into a smile. She wants to know how long until I'll play with her, and if she has to take a nap today. I want to fall asleep when you do, she whispers into my face. I want to wake up when you wake up.

◖

RESEMBLANCES

A squid, like a scholar, disappears behind a cloud of ink.
A housewife, like winter salad, goes down better well-dressed.
Poets, like potatoes, ripen in the dirt.
A divorce lawyer, like a dachshund, digs into deep holes.

O

A Great Book can be read again and again, inexhaustibly, with great benefit to great minds, wrote Mortimer Adler, co-founder of the Great Books Foundation and the Great Books of the Western World program at the university where my husband will be going up for tenure next fall, and where I sometimes teach as well, albeit in a lesser, "non-ladder" position. Not only must a Great Book still matter today, Adler insisted, it must touch upon at least twenty-five of the one hundred and two Great Ideas that have occupied Great Minds for the last twenty-five centuries. Ranging from Angel to World, a comprehensive list of these concepts can be found in Adler's two-volume *Syntopicon: an Index to the Great Ideas*, which was published with Great Fanfare, if not Great Financial Success, by Encyclopedia Britannica in 1952. Although the index includes many Great Ideas, including Art, Beauty, Change, Desire, Eternity, Family, Fate, Happiness, History, Pain, Sin, Slavery, Soul, Space, Time, and Truth, it does not, alas, include an entry on Pillows, which often strike me, as I sink into mine at the end of a long day of anything, these days, as at the very least worthy of note. Among the five hundred and eleven Great Books on Adler's list, updated in 1990 to appease his quibbling critics, moreover, only four, I can't help counting, were written by women—Virginia, Willa, Jane, and George—none of whom, as far as I can discover, were anyone's mother.

O

MISSING SCENES

In which Eve plucks her moustache.
In which Achilles waxes his ass.
In which a butterfly triggers *The Tempest*.
In which Moby Dick performs his own stunts.
In which Bashō smokes hashish.
In which the Buddha buys bonds.
In which the Heavenly Banquet is served with a spork.
In which Galahad chugs from the grail.
In which spring follows summer.
In which moss grows on meteors.
In which Pelé scores on the Peloponnesian Fields.

O

Not in stock, says the campus bookstore clerk looking up from his screen with a smile when I inquire, incognito, after my books, which are nowhere to be found on the shelves. We used to have two copies of the first one, he says, but no one bought them, so we sent them back last June. We never carried the second one, he adds, but we could order it for you. What's your name? I glance up, above his head, at a shelf of Staff Picks. Between a history of disgust and a guide for saving the planet, I spot my husband's last book, gleaming in the day's dying light. Forget it, I mutter into my muffler, I can get it from Amazon by Friday. I go home and order

an ivory satin pillowcase instead, guaranteed to reduce hair loss
due to breakage and soften fine lines.

○

NO USE

Wet cigarettes.
E-cigarettes.
A babysitter whose babysitter is sick.
Nunchucks at a gunfight.
Stiletto heels at the beach.
Last year's flu shot.
Next year's peace talks.

○

Heian courtesans slept lightly, when they slept at all, fully dressed
in perfumed robes on straw mats, behind elaborately painted
screens upon which their noble visitors knocked softly at all hours.
In their onnade "women's script," they kept detailed notes about
flowers, festivals, and furtive trysts on delicately tinted pages
stashed in narrow drawers inside their pillows. These documents,
copied and recopied over the centuries by courtiers, monks, and
scholars in a relentlessly modernizing Japan, provide readers
today with the richest portrait of any culture of its time on the
globe. I now had a vast quantity of paper at my disposal, reports

the nonchalant Shōnagon, and I set about filling the notebooks with odd facts, stories from the past, and all sorts of other things, often including the most trivial material.

○

All day I lie sprawled across my pillow watching a light crust of snow retract across the lawn into a thin band of shade along the fence. I watch the sun fail to rise above the Japanese maple and drop like a coin into a slot in the wall.

○

THERAPIES A TO Z

Art.
Biblio.
Chemo.
Dung.
Electroshock.
Family.
Gestalt.
Hippo.
Ichthyo.
Jenga.
Kite.
Light.

Music.
Neurolinguistic.
Occupational.
Primal scream.
Quantum touch.
Reiki.
Sandplay.
Transpersonal.
Ultraviolet.
Viro.
Wilderness.
X-ray.
Yoga.
Zoo.

◖

Tonight my in-laws dropped by with a rolling suitcase full of silk.
They are back from their fortieth medical school class reunion
in Hyderabad, where they did a little shopping for Her Majesty.
Lehengas, powdas, pull-up saris, scarves, cholis, churidars,
salwar kameez, stoles, and gauzy shawls—a kaleidoscopic array
of embroidered, mirrored, beaded, and beribboned ancestral
confections now lies strewn across the moonlit living room.
Her Majesty, when I check—after a forty-minute meltdown, an
ostensibly unintentional head-butt, a grudging apology, a warm
bath, two books, and three off-key a capella nonconsensual
renditions of *Tomorrow*—lies draped across her pillow in a sky blue
tunic shot with gold. I take a sip of my tepid Neocitrin and close my

eyes. At length I rise from the downy depths of my reverie, gather up the scattered regalia, and stuff the lot as carefully as possible into the large wicker dress-up box in the basement, along with the pink satin Chinese pajamas, plastic King Tut mask, itchy polyester medieval Scottish Disney princess vest, and ever-shifting collection of bangles, boas, Mardi Gras beads, sheriff badges, clown noses, and dollar store crowns.

○

Her Majesty calls me to her bedside in tears, afraid, she maintains, of having a nightmare. This word is a new one for her, and I am concerned, but wary of her infantile tactics. She reminds me of the dream she had last summer, wherein her tattered grey sock puppet, Boxes Rhinoceros, was forced through the keyhole of her door and scattered in pieces across her pillow, the sight of which, I must in fairness concede, wrenched her trembling from sleep in a sweat. That was months ago, I point out. It could happen again, she insists.

○

UNENDURABLE

Writers' conventions.
Old men playing the electric guitar.
Dinner with donors.
Dreadlocks on a WASP.

Group hugs.
Hot pants.
Officious subversives.
Jazz connoisseurs.
A prenatal pole-dancing class.
An undergraduate who has just discovered Foucault.
Ads for Viagra.
Office potlucks.
Thirst.

◐

Some nights she calls out wanting water, or needing to pee. Some nights it's an itch, some nights a bad dream. Some nights I feel my wired mind playing tricks on me, planting her cry inside the white noise on my pillow. Still I grab my robe and stumble into darkness, stubbing my toe on my husband's half-unpacked suitcase by the stairs. Whatever dream I have been plucked from sputters out on the spot like the embers of a campfire dowsed with sand. She does not like me to call her Your Majesty. You are not my servant, she insists crossly but tenderly, before pointing at her pillow on the far side of the room and letting out a soft, majestic sigh.

◐

By the time we die, most of us will have passed a quarter of a century adrift on our pillows, of which six or more years will have been spent in dreams, almost all forgotten upon waking. To ensure better recall, suggests John Glanville, the former born-again Mormon insomniac who once looked Pegasus in the face in a dream and went on to establish the informative online resource dreaminterpretation-dictionary.com, one should supplement one's diet with vitamin B6; drink a full glass of "moonwater"—water, that is, that has been left out in the moonlight overnight for a week—before bed; sleep on a pillow filled with mugwort, borage, lavender, or yarrow; and keep a notebook at the ready beside one's head.

◑

Lady E. from the Autumn Palace in the Western District says I must be sure to include something about Freud in my poem. Maybe you could write it in two parts, she suggests, one about pillows and one about dreams. Since having a baby, I say, I have been abstracted from quiet contemplation and consequently suffer a crippling lack of oneiric recall. As I write, I explain, I am hoping to open things up in my nightlife as well. We squat in my front yard, planting tulip bulbs. One emits a low whirr like a mechanical top and crumbles into dust in my hands. My garden won't grow either, she says. I plant things and they never come up.

●

NO ALTERNATIVE

Landfills.
Tantrums.
Canned peaches in March.
Falling asleep in full make-up while drunk.
Lying to superiors.
Lying to inferiors.
Alternative rock in alternative bars.

●

Nights before I have to teach are the worst. Only my damp, long-suffering pillow stands between me and the dull-witted imposter I will soon publicly be. What dreams do come are dark and brief, and wake me whimpering. Mostly I just lie awake in pre-pedagogical dread. That said, the older I get, the better I become at concealing my fears behind a gay veil of befuddled indifference. It has been some time since a student, more often than not a young man, has corrected my pronunciation of a term in class, or objected to an assignment on theoretical grounds. I no longer precede every session with a furtive slug of whiskey from the glove box or pass from my front door to campus in a cold sweat rehearsing fatuous opening gambits. At least now I am old enough—almost twice the age of most of my students—to feel, with some reason, that even if I am not in fact smarter than they are, thanks to the sheer preponderance of years on my side, I contain a greater volume of knowledge than they do, a fact which surely counts for something, I remind myself often, in the fluorescent bad dream of the classroom. On the other hand, I must also admit that the older I get, the more that knowledge is cancelled out, in effect, by the growing domain of my ignorance.

●

DUBIOUS DOCTORS

Dr. Who.
Dr. No.
Dr. Zhivago.
Dr. Moreau.
Dr. Strangelove.
Dr. Feelgood
Dr. Doolittle.
Dr. Spock.
Dr. Jekyll.
Dr. Faustus.
Dr. Pepper.
Dr. Dre.
Doctors who drink.
Doctors who don't drink.
All Doctors of Literature.

For the first time in six weeks, no mid-level administrators, no visiting scholars, no artists-in-residence, no junior associates, no senior assistants, no mentees, no prospies, and no traveling spouses of acquaintances from college accompanied us on date night, last night. We were alone together, beyond our bolted townhouse door, for the first time since Thanksgiving. Things began on a sweet note. We took the train to a trendy new trattoria in the South Loop. We shared a cigarette under a streetlight in the softly falling snow. We held hands across the table and ordered Whiskey Sours. Things soured, as a result, rather swiftly. The waiter—an impassive, moustachioed hipster with a map of Hades tattooed on his neck—refreshed our empty goblets and withdrew into the shadows with a bow. My husband glowered through his grain-fed-duck-fat fries. I speared my quail confit through angry tears. In a cozy corner booth, a lovestruck couple with thighs entwined under the table hurried through a half-carafe of house red and hustled off into the night without dessert. We downed our dregs in stony silence, and when the candle on our table fizzled out, at ten to ten, we forked over the exorbitant tip, hailed a cab for the extortionate ride down Lake Shore Drive, and shelled out a final fortune to the spent sitter, who was drooling on my pillow in front of *The Bachelorette* when we got home.

●

THINGS THAT GIVE A DIRTY FEELING

Hamsters.
Back-jacket blurbs.
Public pools.
Private school.
Someone else's hairs on the soap.

●

I press my cup against the testy dispenser on the fridge and tinkling cubes tumble down the chute. The kitchen glows. The pillows on our couch have been plumped. Thanks to Estela, who comes every couple of weeks—when she remembers, that is, and can get herself here from across town in her Datsun, which is tired, she explains, and in constant need of repair—I can study my new jowls in the microwave's dust-free mirrored door. Don't get me wrong. I like Estela. What's more, I trust her. I am grateful for the tidy piles of change she arranges by the bed and the gummy earplugs she retrieves from between the sheets. I marvel at the way she combs the snarls out of my hairbrush. No matter how hard I try, for that matter, I cannot master Estela's inimitable technique for balling socks. But it is hard to work, I find, when Estela is here, working so hard—so much harder, to all appearances, than I am—with that smirk of unfathomable peace across her face.

DISHEARTENING

Honorable mention.
Spider veins.
Wet socks.
A half-hearted massage.
No coin for a fountain.
Fine dining at the mall.
Passport pictures.
Petting zoos.
A jukebox full of jazz.

You have gone through four pairs since October, I say. I stitch the fifth pair of mittens to Her Majesty's parka's snotty cuffs. The lone polar bear at the Lincoln Park Zoo, I learn while stirring a pot of day-old oatmeal on the stove, has been removed to a climate-controlled environment indoors. In Michigan, I hear, returning to my pillow for a pre-workout nap, the town of Hell has frozen over and parts of Minnesota are colder than Mars.

◑

Among the Minhe Tu of modern China, if the deceased has enjoyed a natural death—having married, that is, produced healthy offspring and grown old—her head is laid upon a pillow embroidered with a virgin boy and girl extending an embroidered plate of food and flagon of liquor inside a red coffin painted with stars. If her life has failed to meet these minimal requirements, she is thrown into the Yellow River.

◑

Among the Ngoni of modern Tanzania, the feather-stuffed pillow is considered so intimate a possession it is often buried with its owner. When a chief among the Shona of modern South Africa dies, his pillow is passed on to his successor, who prays to it, as to the spirit of his ancestor, in times of crisis before sleep. Among the Luba of the Democratic Republic of the Congo, when the body of the deceased is unavailable for burial, as is often the case given present political realities, his or her pillow is buried instead.

○

UNBEARABLE

The history of Moldova.
The smell of burnt plastic.
Women who wear sexy maid costumes.
Men who suffer women who wear sexy maid costumes.
Rococo decor.
Age thirteen.
The weight of the world.
The lightness of Being.
A tray of "personal effects."

○

Today I spent the morning in the hospital cafeteria, reading about the breakdown of a celebrity marriage in New York. I had been to see the ENT about my sinuses, which the CT scan had shown to be grievously blocked, and stopped on the way out for a coffee and a scone. I took a seat beside the window at a table for six and spread out. I drank three free refills of dark roast and ate a double-chocolate muffin for lunch. Now and then I looked up and cast a cold eye on my companions. An old man hooked to an IV sat wilting in front of his salad, beside a pair of twenty-somethings reading screens. Fit physicians came and went, eating veggie wraps, hiding behind magazines. A heavy-set woman in early middle-age, wearing a hair net and crumpled blue uniform, ate a heaping bowl of carbonara while glaring at the empty seat across from her. I felt calmly, anonymously, at home. I sat there in the thin winter sunlight turning pages, and let their shadows pass over me. An empty wheelchair in the corner, I noticed, when I finally got up to clear my tray and head out, still bore the imprint of a narrow, bony backside on its pillow.

○

Sleep faster, says a Yiddish proverb. We need the pillows.

○

BEAUTIFUL NAMES FOR HIDEOUS THINGS

Chlamydia.
Concertina wire.
Orb Weaver.
White flight.
Night soil.
Crystal meth.
Kristallnacht.
Escargot.
Abattoir.
Apocalypse.
Ambergris.
Ectoplasm.

Strappado.

Lhasa Apso.

Celestial Seasonings Sleepytime Peach Tea.

○

Was she beautiful? She was a favorite at Court, by her own
account anyway. By her own account also, she was past the bloom
of her beauty already, by the time she came to serve the young
Empress. The sole portrait we have is the one she provided from
her pillow in an account of an impromptu visit from a former
lover, the Chamberlain Tadanobu. The plum blossoms in front of
the Palace (red ones on the left and white ones on the right) were
just beginning to scatter, recalls the aging court wit; yet they were
still very beautiful. The sun brilliantly lit up the whole scene—a
scene that I should have liked everyone to view. To make it still
more charming, she continues in her wistful past conditional, the
woman nestling close to the blinds should have been a young lady-
in-waiting with beautiful, long hair cascading over her shoulders.
Instead it was I, an old woman who had long since seen her best
years, and whose hair had become so frizzled and disheveled that
it no longer looked as if it belonged to her head. Alas, there was
not one good thing about me, and I quite spoiled the beauty of
the scene!

O

JOBS FROM HELL

Ingénue Emeritus.
Mother Inferior.
Eternal Finder of the Ragged Edge of Scotch Tape.
Gold digger.
Cat farmer.
Pandemonium Manager.
Plumber to the stars.

O

Wearing a burka and cowboy boots, and pushing a wheel-barrow full of fluorescent lightbulbs through the snow, my best friend from college asks if I object to her mentioning Charles Taylor—the Liberian war criminal, not the analytic philosopher—in front of Her Majesty, or would I prefer that she refer to him simply as "a not nice man." I sit down on a pillow-shaped blob of green Jell-O and think it over. On a hilltop in the distance, a giant Ferris wheel breaks free from its axle, rolls down an empty, winding highway along the crumbling pier towards us, and drops into the ocean at our backs with a splash. A siren sounds in the distance, followed by a chorus of car alarms. I say I am okay with talk about Taylor, I guess, but please go easy on the details.

○

The dream-content is, as it were, presented in hieroglyphics, whose symbols must be translated, one by one, into the language of the dream-thoughts, wrote Freud. My own symbols, when I manage to decipher the nocturnal scribblings in my notebook, seldom pose much of a hermeneutical challenge the next day. A pillow is a pillow is a pillow. A siren, a cry. Wake up.

○

Her Majesty stands over me, grinning excitedly. I was mistaken, apparently, when I complained over drinks last night to the visiting professor from California about the dearth of direct sunlight in our lives. I must now wrench my head from my pillow and follow Her Majesty downstairs. She leads me to the kitchen in silence and stands at the plate glass window facing east. She points to a streak of glowing sky along the low horizon beyond the tracks, and traces with her finger a narrow, golden beam across the floor.

☽

Before streetlights, coffee shops, Costco candles, and Kindles, our species retreated to bed after sunset fully expecting to wake a few hours later for a stretch of dark time. Some filled it with pillow talk, some by reading or writing books. Others visited neighbors, or committed petty crimes. Many babies, to be sure, were planted in that sunless soil between sleeps. Some lay awake contemplating their dreams. Not surprisingly, many prayed. *I am awake,* begins a seventeenth-century British meditation intended for the dead of night, *but 'tis not time to rise, neither have I yet slept enough. I am awake, yet not in paine, anguish or feare, as thousands are.*

◑

Some nights I visit Inés Fernández, the forlorn school teacher from southwestern Spain, who yawned once in the sun at a passing religious procession, felt a brief, searing pain through the back of her skull, and never slept another wink all her life. For the next thirty years she sat up through the night in an armchair in the corner of her bedroom, watching her husband dissolve into dreams in their bed. In the silence and emptiness, she told Rose Grady of *Weekly World News*, I feel as though I am the only person alive in the world. First published on the 23rd of February, 1989, under the headline "Woman Hasn't Slept in Thirty Years!" her grainy portrait still haunts some twilit corner of the internet today. Slumped in a bathrobe in the shadows, her spouse long departed, her thin hair wrenched into an angry topknot on her head, she clutches at the dull, black beads of her rosary and eyes the empty future in grim reprise of the Byzantine Lady of Perpetual Succor framed in dark wood on the wall above her chair. In the foreground, blindly reaching for the viewer from its perch atop a narrow pillow, sits a porcelain infant with its chubby arms outstretched.

NOT RELAXED

Feminists on a list-serv.
Office potlucks.
Endogamy taboos in ancient Greece.
Betty Davis's eyebrows.
Boys at a bris.
Backstage at a folkfest.
Dickinson's dash.

A man is chasing me through a dark house. I do not recognize the furniture, but the staircase in the moonlight, as I hurtle down the banister, looks familiar. The front door, I discover, is bolted shut from the outside. I try the back door, which opens, to my horror, onto a series of inner doors, each smaller than the last, each one shaped like a girl's diminishing silhouette. The final passage is a toddler-sized hatch I must squeeze through as through a swinging doggy door. I hesitate on the threshold, afraid of getting stuck. I am rescued before dawn by Her Majesty climbing beside me into bed, wedging her head next to mine on the pillow and announcing that my nostril breath smells like spaghetti.

●

THINGS THAT ARE DISTANT THOUGH NEAR

Crows on a fence post.
Ex-lovers on Facebook.
Facing-page translations.
Fellow commuters.
Last season's computers.
Yesterday.
Today.

●

THINGS THAT ARE NEAR THOUGH DISTANT

Paradise.
Hell.
The Andromeda Galaxy.
Pen pals.
Laughter on the far side of the bay.

●

The contours of my world, when I compare it to the ancient
watercolor map I find on Wikipedia, would fit very easily within

the gates of Heian-kyō. I live in a tiny pocket of good luck within a blighted urban zone on the South Side of Chicago, in a townhouse a short walk to the University, the grocery store, the preschool, the bank, the emergency room, and the once and future home of the forty-fourth President of the United States of America. Over the past two hundred years, I have learned since we moved here from the North Side, this neighborhood has seen many changes. Some even seem promising. Will the ice cream parlor last? The yoga studio? The cinema? The Chipotle going up in the empty lot behind the liquor store is a good sign. Still, all day at my desk, and on my pillow at night, I hear looping sirens tightening a frail perimeter. I cannot hear the lake, a half-mile to the east, but standing at my window some nights I smell its icy exhalations through the trees.

●

RARE THINGS

Flattering harem pants.
Solitary bedbugs.
Perfect rhymes for *angst*.
A perfectly ripe peach.
Wise fools.
A couple who remember the same fights.

My husband often laughs in his sleep. Sometimes he mutters. Occasionally he carries on a conversation with me for several blissful minutes in his dream. These are mysterious exchanges. His words seem uttered from the far side of the universe. As for me, I often wake drenched in sweat, and flip my pillow over only to discover it hot on both sides. This condition, I have learned, will only worsen as I round the bend toward menopause, a word I cannot utter, I find, without pausing to consider the men who dreamed it up.

Once I shared a plate of sushi with a famous aging editor in New York. He ordered for both of us, impeccably, it seemed to me, if somewhat spartanly. Six pieces of salmon, an avocado roll, extra ginger, and a pot of green tea. Did I have any children, he wanted to know. He was famous for not mincing words. I'd just turned thirty-five and had none. Good, he said firmly. You'll be finished as a writer if you do. The jade green pillows on which we sat, I recall, had been cut from coarse raw silk and embroidered with a vivid black pattern of stars inside a narrow band of chartreuse.

MOUSTACHES A TO Z

Anwar Sadat.
Burt Reynolds.
Che Guevera.
Douglas Fairbanks.
Edgar Allan Poe.
Friedrich Nietzsche.
Gepetto.
Hercule Poirot.
Ivan the Terrible.
Joseph Stalin.
Kim Jong-il.
Leonardo da Vinci.
Mark Twain.
Nebuchadnezzar.
Omar Sharif.
Prince.
Queen Victoria.
Ron Jeremy.
Salvador Dalí.
Teddy Roosevelt.
Usher.
Vlad the Impaler.
Wyatt Erp.
Xerxes.
Yosemite Sam.
Zorba the Greek.

◑

Sleeping nymphs. Nursing Virgins. Enraptured damsels. Tunisian odalisques. Desultory girls draped in curtains and curls. In all the innumerable galleries throughout the art museums of the world, it is hard to find one featuring a pillow that does not also squeeze in a young woman's breast.

◑

Ill-luck upon ill-luck, and a stone for a pillow, says a Spanish proverb. Weariness can snore upon the flint, says Belarius, but resty sloth finds the down pillow hard. A boor remains a boor, says a Danish proverb, even when sleeping on silken pillows.

◑

Move over, I snap at my husband, as I sink beside him into bed. Frowning in his dream, he turns away from me. I snatch my favorite pillow from beneath his sleeping head.

◖

OVER-EAGER

Old men to remember their youth.
Young women to forget their youth.
Doctors to medicate.
Corporations to legislate.
Writers to exchange self-righteous links.

◖

Though my husband insists it's just the soundtrack to the zombie apocalypse he has cajoled me into watching with him, I maintain that the shrieking in the background is coming, in fact, from outside. I crack the sliding back door to confirm. Don't you know this is real, woman? a man bellows beyond the fence. You a fool, a woman's voice rages back, her shadow raising its hands against the neighbors' garage. Put that damn thing down. Call 911, I whisper, frozen stiff on the threshold. But they are on their way already. Within seconds, an unmarked police cruiser glides soundlessly down the dark street, rounds the corner towards the fading cries in the alley, and dissolves into the night like a dream. In the meantime, the motley crew of survivors onscreen, we discover, when we sink back into our pillows with our tepid cups of hot cocoa, have staggered into the temporary safety of a large, abandoned prison farm.

MILITARY OPERATIONS A TO Z

Aloha.
Babylift.
Cobweb.
Dragon's Breath.
Espresso.
Flea Flicker.
Gold Digger.
Hit and Run.
Ithaca.
Just Cause.
King Tut.
Little Man Brief.
Machete Harvest.
Northern Lights.
O.K. Corral.
Paperclip.
Quicksweep.
Rat Trap.
Stocking Stuffer.
Tangerine Squeeze.
Unforgiven.
Vacant City.
Wonderland.
Xcellerator.
Yellow Ribbon.
Zipper.

○

No luck with the potty today, I record in my little blue pillow book. No interest, either, in wearing the new Hello Kitty underwear I bought last week at Target, though Her Majesty did kiss each pair as we removed them from the shiny plastic packaging.

○

From the hovering basket of a hot-air balloon in our front yard, my husband invites a student aboard to discuss her paper on Spinoza. They lift off into a swirling swarm of downy flakes, leaving me behind with Her Majesty in the kitchen, attempting to select, over the telephone, a pair of matching mail-order tattoos. Her Majesty sprawls across a pillow at my feet, scrolling through infinite options onscreen—miles of black and white cartoons of skulls—kitten skulls, puppy skulls, ducklings and bunnies—on the website mommycanigetatattoo.com. The customer service representative grows bored and increasingly abrupt as I stall for more time. I don't know, I say. I was hoping for something more . . . *au courant*? She clears her throat and asks in a strong Southern drawl if I understand the meaning of permanence. In the silence that follows, I hear a bubble pop at the far end of the line.

○

IGNORE AT YOUR OWN RISK

Education.
A train whistle.
A knowing wink from a drunk.
Campus security update alerts.
Warming currents.
Vows made in the dark.

○

If you put a mirror under your pillow, you will dream of the man you will marry. If you pick flowers from a meadow in starry silence at night, and put them under your pillow, you will dream of the man you will marry. If you pluck twelve hairs from your head on New Year's Eve, braid them into a ring, place them into a prayer book at the start of the marriage service, and put it under your pillow, taking care not to speak, and retiring at once, you will dream of the man you will marry. If you dream of taking a bath, you will soon fall in love. To make your lover come to you, sleep with scissors under your pillow.

○

This is corpse sickness, says the illustrious physician Hsu-tsu-po to his ancient patient in the sixteenth century Chinese medical encyclopedia, the *Pen-tsao Kang-mu*. You must go to an old tomb, he advises, and find a pillow with a broken corner. Take the pieces home with you and make a powder from these pieces. Mix the powder with water, and then drink it. The cripple did as she was told and was cured, we are told. We never learn, alas, what did the old woman in, in the end.

○

UNPOPULAR PERFUMES A TO Z

Alimony.
Buffalo Soldier.
Cold Feet.
Dada Dior.
Eau de Angina.
Fat Chance.
Grey Matter.
Happily Married.
Indecision.
Judgment Day.
King's Ransom.
Long Shot.
Money Shot.

Never Mind.
Orientalism 101.
Pay Up Front.
Quandariness.
Rape Me.
SNAFU.
Tryptophantasy.
Uncle.
Vulva-Voom!
Wollstonecraft No.5.
Xtra Pickles.
Yesterday's News.
Zombietown Abattoir Sleepytime Peach Tea.

☾

I tear page after page from my notebook and feed them to my pillowcase, which consumes them, I hear myself saying out loud in the dream, like an unquiet beast.

☾

Psychological Healing Dreams. Belief Dreams. Problem-solving Dreams. Physiological Dreams. Compensatory Dreams. Recurring Dreams. Lucid Dreams. Prophetic Dreams. Nightmares. Dreams of Daily Life. On an ivory stoneware pillow embossed with cracked black lilies from the late Jin dynasty behind glass at the

Art Institute of Chicago, you can still see the murky spectre of the sleeping head that lay there over eight hundred years ago, dreaming the same ten basic dreams we dream today.

○

Many lovers came to see Shōnagon, but few seemed to please her. Those who did, tact prevented her from praising. Anyone turning to her *Pillow Book* in search of courtly dirty-talk or cozy boudoir scenes by candlelight will turn away unsatisfied. The raciest scene in my abridged bedside edition consists of a woman taking a nap alone under bedclothes that smell faintly of sweat. It is, by and large, a dry read. So many Senior Courtiers of the Sixth Rank, Chamberlains of the Right and of the Left, Middle Counselors, Minor Chancellors, and Chancellors' Messengers attend so many Festivals of the Fourth Day of the Fourth Month, of the Eighth Day of the Eighth Month, of the Blue Horses, of the Kamo, and of the Cherry Trees, wearing so many unlined robes of green, yellow, plum, scarlet, crimson, violet, rose, and cherry silk, in palm-leaf and wickerwork carriages, bearing herbal balls, hare-sticks, zithers, and thirteen-pipe flutes, it is hard to endure more than a page or two at a stretch. Therein lies much of its appeal for me. It affords sufficient distraction on one's pillow at night to transport one to a late Kurosawa dream sequence, but also enough repetitive and inconsequential minutiae to conjure, on a good night, the infinitely gentle god of sleep.

◐

NOT TO BE DESPISED

A Hyundai when hitchhiking.
Peanuts when traveling coach.
Support hose at forty.
Dishonorable discharge.
Water from a gas-station sink.

◐

For the third day in a row the doorbell rings just as I am finally settling down to do some work. I resolve to settle the matter once and for all. The man on my stoop holds a shovel in one hand and in the other, his hat. An old pillowcase stuffed with something bulky—empty beer cans?—rests on the welcome mat at his feet. For twenty bucks, he offers to clear the front walk. Behind him, snowy steps descend to an icy path winding between a dead hydrangea and the Subaru parked, as usual, a little too close to the fence. My husband, I recall, will not be home until late. The forecast tonight is more snow. I show the man the contents of my wallet—two crumpled fives and one single—which he accepts, bowing slightly. I nod and withdraw behind the locked door. Eleven dollars, I reflect as I return to the keyboard with my tepid kombucha, isn't bad for a half-hour's effort. If he works fast, he could be done in twenty minutes. When I take a cupcake break in the kitchen moments later, however, I spy him out the sliding glass door, dragging his shovel behind him down the street, my icy walkway, to all appearances, untouched. Fair enough, I say, jangling my pajama pocket full of loose change.

Pillow is a funny word, Her Majesty announces in the rosy glow of her nightlight. So is *Word*. She sits up wide-eyed and smiles. *Word* is a funny word, she repeats. So is *Funny*! So is *Goodnight*, I intone from the doorway, and dissolve in the dark.

GUILTY PLEASURES

Beating a child at checkers.
Peeing in swimming pools.
Watching *Dateline*.
Drinking milk from the carton.
Glimpsing one's neighbor at home in her curlers.
Glimpsing one's neighbor at home in her curlers, watching
    Dateline, drinking milk from the carton.
A roaring fire in July.

QUESTIONABLE GESTURES

To haggle with hookers.

To roast a bride.

Tax-deductible gifts.

To supplement a hunger strike with juice.

A post-doc at Yale School of Medicine's Center for Obesity
Research sponsored by Pizza Hut.

Golden parachutes.

Faux fur.

Blush on a corpse.

Last night I had a dream so vivid I didn't bother to record it on
my pillow. I was sipping a large stein of sangria at some sort of
nightmarish gala, leaning on the arm of a once-powerful older
man I'd met in college, upon whom I was now, in the dream,
in the awkward position of passing literary judgment. He was
wearing a white guayabera shirt with pink stitching, and what hair
of his remained was slicked across a forehead speckled with age.
I woke angry and aroused and could not get back to sleep. Was
this a Prophetic Dream? A Psychological Healing Dream? A Belief
Dream? The only option I could rule out for certain was a Dream
of Daily Life.

●

INCONGRUOUS

A vegan in Vegas.
A poor plastic surgeon.
Tempests with names like "Trudy" and "Ted."
Perfume at a funeral.
Military dolphins.
Black balloons.
Light rock.

●

I read a message last night from a woman I have yet to meet beyond the dim glow of a list-serv. She lives in Tampa, if memory serves, and won a juried prize last year for a mixed-media meditation on habitat loss across America, including charts, chants, photographs, oral histories, crowdfunded films, and salvaged trash. She tracks the migratory patterns of purple martins above Wal-Mart parking lots and graphs the spawning grounds of Northern leopard frogs from the Gulf Stream waters to the redwood forests. She posts quarterly reports on her blog. She now finds herself, she confessed last night, in the unfamiliar position of lacking words. While dropping off her child at preschool yesterday, she explained, she learned from a social worker stationed in the foyer about the sudden death, on Wednesday night, of a boy in the class. An accident at home, is all she knows. The details remain undisclosed.

The toddlers have been told that their friend now lives inside their hearts. What does that mean, her daughter wants to know. What does it mean that he is *in* our hearts? She doesn't want Sam inside her, her daughter insists. Sam picks his nose. She doesn't want Sam's boogies polluting her heart. At a loss for words myself, I don't reply. I sit at Her Majesty's bedside that night and watch snowy pillows pile up on the peeling deckchairs outside.

●

BETTER BY MOONLIGHT

Equestrian statues.
Landfills.
The Grand Canyon.
Sex after forty.
Lawn furniture.
Travel plans.
Beethoven's *Moonlight Sonata*.

●

The skeleton of the stocky, sixteen-year-old Neanderthal boy known to us as Le Moustier was discovered curled on its side in the fetal position in the dim glow of a cave in Peyzac-le-Moustier, France, in 1908 AD. Beside his dusty remains, over forty-five thousand years old, lay a small handaxe and the scattered bones of wild cattle. Miraculously intact, the boy's toothy skull, with its lumbering brow-ridge and sloping forehead, rested on a small, undisturbed cairn of ancient stones. His bones were promptly sold for a handsome fee by an amateur Swiss fossil hunter and suspected German spy to the Museum für Völkerkunde in Berlin, where all but his badly damaged cranial remains were destroyed in the flames of World War II. Le Moustier's pillow, which as far as I can discover is the oldest one known on Earth, has not survived. The foxes have their holes, the birds of the air have their nests, but the Son of Man hath no place to lay his head, says Jesus in the Gospel According to Luke.

◐

The pillow has a certain sacredness, reports Lafcadio Hearn, also known in some circles as Koizumi Yakumo, in his 1894 account of life in the Far East, *Glimpses of Foreign Japan*. Only this I know, that to touch it with the foot is considered very wrong; and that if it be kicked or moved thus even by accident, the clumsiness must be atoned for by lifting the pillow to the forehead with the hands, and replacing it in its original position respectfully, with the word "gomen," signifying I pray to be excused.

◐

There's a word for this era we live in, I am reminded one midnight on my pillow in a *New York Times* "Opinionator" column I find by following a link on my youngest-living unmarried ex-boyfriend's brother's friend's Facebook wall. The Anthropocene, I recall, is a term that reminds us we are living in an epoch—rapidly coming to a close, many authorities agree—marked by the arrival of the human species as a geohistorical force. The biggest problem we face, opines the column's author, Roy Scranton, a Shock and Awe veteran now pursuing a doctoral degree in English Literature at Princeton, is not one of survival, but of understanding—as did the eighteenth-century Japanese samurai-turned-monk, Yamamoto Tsunetomo—that we are already dead.

◑

THINGS THAT HAVE LOST THEIR POWER

Breast implants.
Body counts.
Heroic couplets.
Caged whales.
Standing ovations.
The League of Nations.
The United Nations.
Nations.
Polio.
Priests.
Pennies.
Theories of power.

◐

THINGS THAT WILL NEVER LOSE THEIR POWER

Hemorrhoids.
Hurricanes.
Puppies.
Flags.
Gossip.
Vodka.
Windmills.
Worms.

◐

I show up late to a party on the lawn of a large, mid-century modern estate. People stand around in small groups, sipping cocktails in the sun. My parents, stone-faced and silent behind a sliding glass door, eye my oldest-living ex-boyfriend guzzling a glass of champagne by the gate while my husband, looking painfully away, distracts Her Majesty with a large hand puppet in the shape of a human heart. I make a beeline for the bathroom inside, at the end of a long, wood-paneled hall, past a bedroom piled high with satin cushions like the ones tossed back and forth between Rock Hudson and Doris Day in the opening credits of *Pillow Talk*. Before the blinding white console, my foundation spills all over the little black dress I have borrowed from a narrower friend. I sit down to pee without closing the stall. A young woman I recognize, a former advisee, emerges from a room across the hall and sees me. I explain that I don't usually leave the door open like this, and then laugh and say sadly, actually, I do.

O

To divert the tempest brewing in her bloodstream I agree to buy Her Majesty the item of her choice. We have driven through a blizzard to a drafty craft emporium for supplies to repurpose, with the aid of glue and "magic," into valentine cards for her classmates. Tomorrow, I recalled at three a.m. today, is the fourteenth. Her Majesty bolts down aisle thirteen. I dash after, past racks packed with baskets, papier-mâché puppy masks, stacks of Styrofoam hats. I pass a Sears Tower of popsicle sticks, sacks of cellophane snow, and wind through a vast, frozen, parti-colored forest of plastic flowers beneath a frozen flock of paper birds. When I finally discover her, deep inside a costume rack, Her Majesty refuses to be parted from a spangled tiara affixed to a diaphanous cascade of ivory foam. I steer her towards a litter of pink kittens made of pom-poms from a kit. I point out a pony she can tar with rainbow glitter and gold fluff. She smiles and clutches at the gauzy white stuff of her dreams. At night from the hallway, through a narrow crack in her door, I watch with dumb care her infinite care as she lies down on her pillow so as not to disturb a single flawless faux rose.

○

HARDER THAN IT LOOKS

IKEA.
Green grass.
Small talk with a psychoanalyst.
Metaphysics for Dummies.
Two in a hammock.
A perfect circle.
A hard look.

○

The grandmother of a classmate of Her Majesty's stopped me on the street today. She had just come from the park, she said, where Her Majesty was playing with her nanny, and she sincerely hopes I know how lucky I am. I assured her I do. Precious indeed are the hours I have passed, downstairs in my study or outside on the patio with a smoke, oblivious to first steps, tantrums, playdates, and picnics, stopping up my ears against Her Majesty's cries, secure in the knowledge that wherever she is, and whatever she is doing, Her Majesty is in the loving care of an uncanonized Puerto Rican saint. But it is not always easy, I did not say to the stranger, to be a saint's patron. When I forget to pay her wages, I did not say, for example, she just smiles and says nothing, causing no small inconvenience for my husband who insists on driving across town to pay up the next day. When I forgot her birthday, her daughter's quinceañera, and the final performance of the Nutcracker downtown to which I had promised to take them as a holiday treat, I did not say, she forgave me with the same patient look in her eyes that always cuts me to the quick. What's more, I did not mention, she receives my spontaneous gifts, many of which, I trust she appreciates, represent a considerable expenditure on my part, with such glacial reserve that it is often impossible to tell if she is genuinely pleased. Sometimes she neglects to mention them at all, which I find awkward in the extreme. Did you like the glass teapot? The framed poster of the blue-morpho butterfly? Are you fond of the throw pillows with matching afghan and slippers? Needless to say, one does not like to have to ask.

○

Was Shōnagon bored? Was she lonely? Her correspondence, which must have been copious, has not survived. Her pillow book focuses almost exclusively on impressions and anecdotes past. She seldom speaks of the present, and never mentions future plans. She does not, as far as I can discover, record a single dream or nightmare that visited her in sleep, nor does she mention the son or daughter she is rumored to have borne. She does, however, permit herself one brief flight of fancy throughout the several hundred entries in my bedside edition. I should like to live in a large, attractive house, she begins, in her translator's upright subjunctive. My family would of course be staying with me; and in one of the wings I should have a friend, an elegant lady-in-waiting from the Palace, with whom I could converse. Whenever we wished, we should meet to discuss recent poems and other things of interest. When my friend received a letter, we should read it together and write our answer. Whenever my friend went to the Palace, I should help her with her preparations and see that she had what was needed during her stay. For everything about well-born people delights me. But, concludes the well-born court has-been in lighthearted haste, I suppose this dream of mine is rather absurd!

○

Consider, meanwhile, the case of Thai Ngoc, a low-born farmer from Quang Nam Province, Vietnam, who was wrenched from his pillow by a fever at the age of thirty-one and for the past forty years has remained in a state of perpetual alertness on his commune, digging fish ponds by moonlight, planting sugar cane, and guarding houses during funerals so the families of the dead can get some rest. Known around the world as the Man Who Could Not Sleep, by day he continues his work in the fields, walking home every evening down the two-mile footpath with two hundred-pound sacks of pig feed on his back. His six children live with him, along with his wife, who discussed her husband's unfathomable condition in an interview with *Thanh Nien News* in 2006. My husband used to sleep well, she confided, but these days, even liquor cannot put him down.

O

DRINKING GAMES A TO Z

Aunt Sally.
Boot of Beer.
Centurion.
Dizzy Bat.
Edward Fortyhands.
Fuzzy Duck.
Goon of Fortune.
Hammershlagen.
Ice Luge.
Jenga.
Kings.
Liar's Dice.
Matchbox.
Never Have I Ever.
Odd Man Out.
Power Hour.
Quarters.
Ride the Bus.
Shut the Box.
Three Man.
Up Jenkins.
Vanishing Cups.
Waterfall.
Xeno's Paradox.
Yard of Ale.
Zip Zap Zop.

O

We crowd on throw pillows and stools around a Formica table drinking sake. A storm rattles the fire escape. A water heater clangs in a far-away wall. Someone tells a story from his childhood about playing soccer in falling snow on a dirt field flanked by tanks. Another recalls being struck by a Jeep and waking up in the E.R. covered in mud. A silky Persian emerges from the bathroom, leaps onto the table and is shooed off. Someone recounts the incident in Chekhov she always thinks of when she sees a grey cat. I gorge myself on pickled vegetables, pots of broth, egg pancakes, and heaping plates of grilled meats. As our host is refilling my raised cup, I finally break my silence to remark that I've been reading a wonderful history of medieval Japan. My host, who is Korean, smiles benignly.

O

NOT FRENCH

French's French Fried Onion Chicken.
My French accent.
Paris Hilton.
French Guiana.
Rap music.
Paris, Texas.
The Paris Hilton.
Celestial Seasonings Sleepytime Peach Tea.

◗

Slowly a globe assembles itself in Her Majesty's head. It bears little resemblance to the globe in my head, but there are points of convergence. She has begun to draw maps—tangled networks of lines called Chicago, My Bedroom, Upstairs, India, Today, and Outside. One morning before dawn she calls me to her pillow to tell me there are countries in the world with no dolls. Like where? I ask. She considers. Like here, she says, but without any dolls.

◗

BETTER IN GERMAN

Kindergarten.

◗

BETTER IN FRENCH

Abattoir.

BETTER IN JAPANESE

Throne of Blood.

BETTER IN PERSIAN

Shock and Awe.

BETTER IN PICTURES

Stonehenge.

BETTER IN THE ABSTRACT

Abstract art.

Within a ten minute walk from my pillow is Jackson Park, site of the 1893 World's Columbian Exhibition and host in its glory to over fifteen hundred visitors a day. Today it hides in plain sight like a bright slice of enlightenment, host to a striking variety of migrating songbirds, wintering waterbirds, endless waves of incontinent geese, and a small night heron who hugs the muddy shore of the Osaka Garden pond, which was destroyed by patriotic vandals during World War II and restored reluctantly fifty years later with municipal funds. I like to walk there when the sun is out. One day I brought pillows and sat in the gazebo with Her Majesty, sipping Celestial Seasonings Sleepytime Peach Tea.

●

Not a memoir. Not an epic. Not a scholarly essay. Not a shopping list. Not a diary. Not an etiquette manual. Not a gossip column. Not a prayer. Not a secret letter sent through the silent palace hallways before dawn. Lacking as it does a table of contents, an index, plot, or any discernible chronology or structure, with almost a thousand pages of surviving material, translated, retranslated, and republished in ever-shifting editions, what are the chances, I sometimes wonder, that any two people ever read the same *Pillow Book*?

ALTERED PROVERBS

People who live in glass houses should install blinds.
Home is where the Walmart is.
Where there's a will there's a lawsuit.
Let she who is without sin take the first bong hit.
In the kingdom of the blond the albino is king.
Two in the bush is better than nothing.
If you lie down with poets, you will get up with fleas.
When in Rome stay at the Ritz.
The road to hell wasn't built in a day.
Oil and water make the world go round.
The grass is always greener over graves.
To forgive is human, to forget divine.
A journey of a thousand miles begins when the fat lady sings.
Truth is stranger than the sum of its parts.

A broken pencil, a whistle, a plastic harmonica, beach glass, ribbon, a Hello Kitty Halloween vampire bat sticker, and most recently the broken heel of the purple plastic high heel princess shoe her grandmother caved in and bought her last summer figure prominently among the endlessly rotating assortment of talismans I find beneath Her Majesty's pillow. Some nights I try to imagine the whole collection.

The Brookstone Biosense Memory Foam Shoulder Pillow. The Sleep Innovations Gel Memory Foam Contour Pillow. The Viscofresh Advanced Contour Memory Foam Classic Pillow. The Serta Reversible Gel-Memory Foam Classic Pillow. The Dream Form Ventilated Jumbo-Sized Memory Foam Neck Pillow. The AB Marketers Deluxe Memory Foam Ultra-plush Lumbar Pillow. The Sensorpedic Basic Dual Comfort Standard Gusseted Memory Foam Shoulder Pillow. The Carpenter Co Perfect Luxury Gusset Pillow. The Dream Form Memory Foam Latex and Microfiber Dupont Polyester Down-Alternative-Fill Pillow.

Pillows, I say, when people ask what I'm writing about, which occurs all too rarely. It's a book about someone who can't sleep, I explain, who's writing a book about pillows. The more pillows I write, however, the more strongly I suspect that what I'm writing about pillows is as much about pillows as last night's dream about getting lost in an underground parking lot at the mall was about getting lost in an underground parking lot at the mall.

◐

IMPOSSIBLE

To conquer Prussia.
To view Paul Klee's complete works.
To taste the word "apple."
To ride the Trojan Horse.
To sleep through *Meatballs*.
To stay awake through *Swan Lake*.
To relax with a traffic cop.
To wind a lost watch.
To summer in Paris without stepping in shit.
To eat a Happy Meal without feeling depressed.
To fish the Sea of Tranquility.
To film a dream.
To weigh a shadow.
To surprise a fire.

◐

BITTERSWEET

Organ donations.
Negronis.
The skin of a plum.
Floral gum.
Deadly Nightshade.

Psychoactive toads.
Free coffee at the bank.
Pillow talk while drunk.

◐

Every day for five years, laughs my mother, who has been married to my father for forty-eight years, when I ask her from my pillow one morning if, when I was small, she ever considered leaving my father.

◐

There are times when the world so exasperates me, recalls Shōnagon, that I feel I cannot go on living in it for another moment and I want to disappear for good. But then, if I happen to obtain some nice white paper, Michinoku paper, or white decorated paper, I decide that I can put up with things as they are a little longer. Or, if I can spread out a finely woven, green straw mat and examine the white bordering with its vivid black patterns, I somehow feel that I cannot turn my back on this world, and life actually seems precious to me. We have Her Majesty, the lovely Empress Sadako, who died in childbirth at the age of twenty-four, to thank for keeping her petty courtesan's pillow, however briefly, supplied with nice white paper, Michinoku paper, and white decorated paper.

O

I stroll through a wonderland of waterfalls and ponds, wooden footbridges, lush clusters of ferns and bonsai pines. A miniature mountain rises serenely in the mist beyond a grassy field on which tea has been set out before a pair of moonlit pillows. It is my thesis defense. I have been hard at work for many years, and finally completed it. Here it is, I announce, turning exultantly to see my husband's beaming face. I see in his eyes right away, I have made a terrible mistake. My examiner, a stylish colleague exactly my age tenured two years early last fall for her cutting-edge work on sinking cities, emerges from the bushes with a clipboard, eyebrow raised. She smiles from behind red Lucite glasses and offers me a small, ceramic figurine, unearthed, she explains, over a thousand years ago on Pluto. It's purely ornamental, she adds, of no use to her, or to anyone serious.

O

Life in medieval Japan, needless to say, was not all perfume and pillow talk. Thanks to a bumper crop of epidemics—measles, mumps, malaria, smallpox, dysentery, beriberi, tuberculosis, and influenza—to say nothing of the diabetes and mysterious cardio-pulmonary infirmities that plagued the inbred oligarchy, along with rice famine, on the average, every three years, widespread warfare in the provinces, frequent cyclones and typhoons, and the constant risk of fires due to the perilous convergence of bamboo roofs, paper walls, floor-length robes, and fragile oil lamps, the average life span in medieval Japan was twenty-seven, if you were female, or thirty-two, if you were not. Ghosts were rampant, baths rare; birth was accompanied by ceaseless chanting of spells. The baby's chances of surviving her fifth birthday, in Shōnagon's day, were fifty-fifty at best. Was she frivolous? Sei herself, rumor has it, lived past forty. In one account, she meets with a solitary death in Buddhist rags. In another, she's rewarded with a high official for a husband and a daughter who grows up to serve at court. Some nights I try to imagine Option C.

○

FIRST WORLD PROBLEMS A TO Z

Abstract art.
Blackout blinds.
Chemotherapy wigs.
Divorce court.
Existential philosophy.
Foreign rights.
Gap year blues.
Homebirth rallies.
Income tax.
Jet lag.
Kindergarteners carrying heavy wifi loads.
Lunch-truck fatigue.
Metacriticism.
Non-communicable, age-related cardio-pulmonary diseases.
Orthodontists.

Peckishness.

Quandariness.

Retro-modern décor ennui.

Second World problems.

Third World problems.

Under-enrolled inner-city charter schools.

Vanity publishing.

Weltshmerz.

Xfinity router outages.

Yoghurt packaging rage.

Zero money down.

○

The most common of all sleep disorders, insomnia afflicts at least a third of all Americans, to say nothing of the hundreds of millions of undocumented zombies worldwide. Despite extensive research funded by such august institutions as the Harvard Clinical and Translational Science Center, the American Academy of Sleep Medicine, the European Sleep Research Society, the South African Society of Sleep, the Brazilian Sleep Foundation, the Cairo Center for Sleep Disorders, the Japanese Society of Sleep Research, the Indian Board of Sleep Medicine, the Sino-German Sleep Medicine Cooperation, the Russian Society of Somnologists, the World Sleep Federation, and the International Institute of Sleep, however, this global affliction remains etiologically and pathogenetically elusive, at best. One problem, suggest specialists, among whom I can only imagine must number at least a handful of indefatigable investigators, is that the majority of sufferers radically underestimate both the quality and quantity of their sleep. Insomnia, after all, like boredom and pain, is a subjective complaint, not to be confused with its nastier, "objective" cousin, sleep deprivation, which has other causes, consequences, and clinical presentations altogether. If an insomniac claims to drowse two or three fitful hours on her pillow, studies find, she has probably passed, in perfect peace, at least twice that time.

○

I stand at the railing of a cruise ship with my friend. Bright scenery floats past us on vast screens. It's the Mexico of India, I say, gesturing to the candy-colored slums crowding a nearby riverbank. On a set of wide concrete steps descending into the water, bony children in rags toss bloody strips of meat into the jaws of waiting crocodiles, who snap at their bare feet. Her Majesty, I am troubled to discover, is among them, and does not look up when I call out to her. It does not seem like a good idea to me to let small children play with large reptiles, I remark, but my friend is gone, and in her place stands a wilting potted palm. The ship takes a hairpin turn down a snow-covered alley and emerges a school bus. Out the rear window I watch Her Majesty, trailed by the slavering lizards, recede through the heavy iron doors of a concrete mausoleum, which swing shut just as I reach them. I hear an icy scream from within, and feel a man's hand on my shoulder reaching out to catch me in mid-collapse. I turn on my pillow to find my husband, still asleep, fumbling at the neck of my pajamas in a dream.

○

Men and women sleep on the same pillow, says a Mongolian proverb, but they have different dreams.

○

If a man sees himself eating crocodile meat: good, it means becoming an official among his people. If a man sees himself measuring barley in a dream: bad, it means the rising of words against him. If a man sees himself burying an old man: good, it means prosperity. If a man sees himself in a mirror in a dream: bad, it means finding another wife. If a man sees himself seeing the moon shining: good, it means a pardon from god. If a man sees himself removing the nails of his fingers: bad, this means removal of the work of his hands. This dream book in the hand of Qenherkhepeshef, the royal scribe to Ramses the Great, circa 1278-1212 BC, removed from his step-son's eternal bedroom in the Valley of Kings circa 1949 AD, along with fragments of a pillow bearing a spell for good sleep in the Western District for the Justified—the oldest living euphemism for the dead—may be viewed upon request, by the inquisitive visitor, at the British Museum where it currently rests.

O

EXTINCT LANGUAGES A TO Z

Akkadian.
Beothuk.
Ceylon Portuguese.
Dalmatian.
Emok.
Fecakomodiyo.
Gafat.
Hadramautic.
Iazychie.
Judeo-Piedmontese.
Kaffir.
Labanki.
Mahican.
Norn.
Old Church Slavonic.
Pannonian Romance.
Qatabanian.
Rafaelii.
Skepi Creole Dutch.
Trojan.
Upper Umpqua.
Vandalic.
Wappo.
Xakriabá.
Yugh.
Zhang-Zhung.

◑

The oldest living dead words in the world today amount to lists scratched into clay by Sumerian scribes circa 3100-2900 BC in the ancient Mesopotamian city of Uruk, now in modern Iraq. Among the many fine examples of these precious "pillow-tablets"—on permanent display in the Ancient Near Eastern Gallery at the Metropolitan Museum of Art in New York City—is a rectangular grey slab no larger than a smart phone which depicts, in the austere, jaunty, orientalist style of Paul Klee, an administrative account concerning malt and barley groats.

◑

Sandstone. Limestone. Terracotta. Jade. Granite. Ivory. Alabaster. Brass. Porcelain. Iron. Cherry-wood. Glass. No evidence suggests that pillows fashioned from such materials were more comfortable in the past than today.

◑

A human pillow is a shifting pillow, warns an old Maori proverb. A pillow of earth, that's the pillow that lasts.

◐

Why Shōnagon? asks a wizened monk in a vintage Benihana hat sharpening his knives in the front row. A murmur rumbles through the conference room. Out the window, a solitary black pine twists against a watercolor wind. On a folding chair in the corner, looking bored and vaguely hostile, like a night guard at a shopping mall, sits a massive biomorphic pillow with sky blue eyes. When I smile, it shows its teeth. I mean, my inquisitor inquires, plucking a paper fan out of the air beside his head and giving it a flick of the wrist, who do you think you are? Um, I stammer into the microphone, which turns into a pair of melting ivory chopsticks in my hand, could you repeat the question in Japanese? Origami cranes rain from the rafters. The floorboards soften into wet grass. I step back from the podium and look down. I am barefoot, I see. Henna paisleys my extremities. My torso bulges from the itchy red silk wedding sari I have on in the picture above my in-laws' couch. The safety pins pop open at my armpits and hips. Turning to run, I wake up twisted in the sheets.

◐

Looking up from the empty, plastic squeeze-bottle she has swaddled in a dishtowel, pillowed on a folded sheet of bubble wrap, and tucked into a shoebox in the corner of the kitchen while I cook, Her Majesty breaks off her singing and scowls. Why does the bough break, she asks crossly. I chop the end off an onion and smile. That's how the song goes, I say breezily. Why does the baby fall, she persists. Does the baby *die* when she falls? I mince the onion into a heap and look up. It's possible, I venture cheerfully. But most people live until they're very, very old and their bodies wear out and they are ready to transform into something new and beautiful, I explain, waving my knife in a circular motion in the air. I scrape the onion into the pot and watch it sizzle in smoking oil. Like flowers or rainbows or puppies or stars, I suggest. But first they have to die, Her Majesty continues, undeterred, and not be what they are. I sprinkle salt into the pot and watch it dissolve. Nothing ends, I say brightly. Everything keeps changing from one thing into another, over and over throughout all space-time. I smile. I dump a cup of diced carrots into the mix. Oh, she says thoughtfully, looking down at her faceless squeeze-bottle baby. Like recycling, she says. Exactly, I say, stirring in the hot chicken stock I've boiled down from last night's bones.

●

Dutifully observing the first cardinal rule of proper sleep hygiene—no screens in bed—I carry my iPad and earbuds down the hall through the dark and curl up in the powder blue polka dotted rocker beside Her Majesty's bed to binge-watch *The Good Wife* on Netflix. By the dim glow of my screen, I watch three back-to-back episodes before looking up to watch Her Majesty's ribs' soft fall and swell under the sheet, which slips away to reveal a bare foot. Her face is turned away from me, half-buried in her pillow, the far side smothered in a snarl of dark curls. I hear the soft smack of her infantile lips, suckling at the infinite. I lie down beside her and inhale the sweet funk of her neck. All kamma is resolved and the mind-flower of wisdom blooms in Nibbàna's eternal spring. Somewhere in the gathering dawn beyond the blinds, the first car alarm of March hails the sun.

●

May the pigeons awaken you when you are asleep, may they awaken your head at the horizon. Raise yourself, so that you may be triumphant over what was done against you, for Ptah has felled your enemies, and it is commanded that action be taken against those who would harm you. You are Horus, son of Hathor, the male and female fiery serpents, to whom was given a head after it had been cut off. Your head shall not be taken from you afterwards, your head shall not be taken from you for ever. Despite this spell from the Book of the Dead recited at his funeral and inscribed in hieroglyphs on a pillow in his tomb, the cranium of young Tutankhamun of the Nineteenth Dynastic New Kingdom was removed from his body by the British archeologist Howard Carter in 1922 AD, in order to extract it from the coffin into which it had been glued.

●

I descend underground in an elevator and emerge on an empty subway platform. A train waits with doors open. I board an empty car, walk its length, and emerge moments later through the open rear doors before the train pulls away from the station. I wake up placid on my pillow, and wonder if this counts as a Problem-solving Dream. I finally fall back asleep and am roused before dawn by the sound of a cricket chirping loudly in my chamber, only to discover that my husband has reset, yet again, the ringtone of his bedside alarm.

●

SOUNDS I DON'T EXPECT TO HEAR

Solar wind.
A rose opening.
Silence on the 4th of July.
The mating cry of the King Island Emu.
Hecklers at the ballet.
Foghorns in the Mare Cognitum.
Melting cheese.
A rich man entering Heaven.
A poor man entering the Senate.
Mermaids singing.
Pure math.

●

We are already dead, I repeat, as I punch down my pillow. We are dead, I say, as I bunch up the sheets. We are dead, I sigh, as I study the back of my husband's head. I stare at the ceiling. I count to six and sit up. We are already dead, I say, as I pour another cold bowl of Kashi with milk. I bow over the sink in a pool of orange light. Her Majesty's construction paper pinwheel crookedly spins on the front lawn. We are dead, sings the wind. We are dead, sings the wheel. We are dead, I repeat the next day in my head, as we hurtle downhill on a blue plastic sled.

●

THINGS THAT MAKE THE HEART BEAT FASTER

Applause.
Raccoons on the roof.
A backwards glance on the street.
Sleeping babies.
The telephone ringing in the dark.

●

I stand before a glowing glass case in the Asian wing. Before me, outstretched at eye-level on white linen, a plump boy in yellow robes lies on his side, clutching a swan to his breast. A tight green cap, not unlike the one Her Majesty wears, under protest, to swimming class, has been smoothed over his ears. Time has flaked the glaze from his face, exposing grey patches of ceramic underneath. Does he remember me? His eyebrows, gently arched, lend him an air of infinite indifference, as does the infinitesimal grin on his lips. I failed to notice this, the last time I looked at him, twelve years ago, if memory serves, which admittedly it seldom does. Even the thousand-year-old swan looks new to me. The stone boy forgets nothing. His right iris, worn to the milky pearlescence of a dead star, stares coolly beyond history. Along the outstretched length of his left flank, balanced on his shoulder and hip, rests a scalloped headrest of smooth, jade-color clay that looks to me about as forgiving as a tombstone on a battlefield, but is identified on the plaque as a cloud. By way of a pillow, the boy himself makes do with the stony folds of his sleeve.

●

The history of pillows begins in the grave. Toys, tools, armies, books, chariots, banquets, bangles, and wives—among the rich array of buried assets excavated from across Earth's vast necropolis, no item turns up more consistently. Today these grave goods, as the archeologists call them, are the only traces left of ancient sleep. It exhausts me to look at them. It fatigues me to spend my days reading and thinking and writing about them, in lieu of nobler or more profitable pursuits, without hope, for that matter, of ever solving sleep's riddle. When I lie awake in the dim glow of my chamber and contemplate these otherworldly objects carved from onyx, whale bone, hippopotamus ivory, rose wood, marble, gold, and turquoise glass; shaped like boats, beans, clouds, oxen, houses, babies, boxes, carriages, and drums; stained with pollen, blood, sweat, goats' urine, and tears; tucked into dim drawers in the earth for all eternity and then dug up and displayed for a brief spell behind glass—the same brief spell I inhabit—I feel as though I am the dark residue of someone's dream. Sleeping Tiger. Porcelain Phoenix. Bucephalo-Phallic Plough. Solar Barque. Boy-Shaped Pillow. Cloud-Shaped Pillow. Pillow in the Shape of a Boy Supporting a Cloud-Shaped Pillow.

◑

Inside the Kagawa Prefectural Museum of History in the ancient city of Kagawa, Japan, on the southern shore of the Seto Inland Sea, rests a funerary pillow from the Fifth or Sixth century AD that looks carved from a black slab of time. Shaped like a shoe for some colossal, mythic steed, it cradles the ghost of a king's noble head inside a smooth, polished hollow at its core. Its inner edge, haloing the long-vanished skull, is pierced with narrow holes which appear to have been used, reports the small silver plaque at its base behind glass, to attach long-vanished stone flowers.

◑

DREAM INTERPRETATIONS

If you dream of a cruise ship, an iceberg is melting.
If you dream of Kraft Dinner, you will see a torn flag.
If you dream about wind chimes, a neighbor's home will collapse
    in the spring.
All soldiers mean travel.
A closed book means nothing.

An open book means you will soon see a ghost.

If you dream about horseflies, houseguests are coming.

If you dream about houseguests, houseguests are coming.

If you dream about drinking, your in-laws will arrive with bad news from the east.

A polar bear means conflict on a list-serv or an over-crowded bus or a heartfelt robo-call from the Vice President's wife.

A construction site is a root canal.

A root canal is an IRS audit or a preschool fundraiser bakesale or a LinkedIn request from an ex or a day-trip in the rain to the zoo.

If you smoke in a dream, your mother will call.

If you drown in a dream, you will dream about smoking.

If your computer screen freezes, you will dream about drones while you flip through *Siempre Mujer* with your mouth stuffed with gauze.

A tulip bulb is a deadline.

Worms are students and students are worms.

All exes are outstanding debts.

If you dream you are leading a group of famous Egyptologists through the hieroglyphs in the Valley of Kings, you will soon win a game of Trivial Pursuit.

A broken boot heel means death or a dropped call.

A bent fork means rain.

If you dream you are running, your credit card will be declined on the birthday of someone you love at the mall.

If you dream of winter, spring is coming.

If you dream of spring, winter is coming.

If you dream you are writing, you are not writing.

◑

A carriage pulls up and I step in, taking care to lift my perfumed hair over the soiled iron threshold. I spot an unclaimed pillow with a painted gold chrysanthemum, and take a seat among several shadowy figures in the gloom. As my eyes begin to adjust, I make out the pale faces of an Intendant of the Office of Palace Works, a low-ranking Senior Courtier, a Chamberlain of the Fifth Rank, the Chancellor, the Emperor, and the Emperor's small dog, Okinamaru, clearly overdue for a bath, who leaps at once into my lap and begins to lick the powder off my chin, causing my companions to smile into their sleeves and look away. The ringing of the temple gong echoes in my ears as though I were sitting at the bottom of a well. The carriage rumbles on for many years over boulders and roots in its path, and finally comes to a stop in the middle of a flooded rice field. I step down and remove a paper fan from my robes. I stand there in the moonlight, ankle deep in the mud, opening and closing my fan, lost in contemplation among the delicate clouds hand-painted by Her Majesty that drift across its infinite folds.

◑

If you wish to rise early, ask your pillow to wake you. Tell it exactly what time you wish to wake up and repeat your request politely three times. Go directly to sleep, taking care not to utter another word before your head touches down. In the morning you will wake well-rested, at precisely the hour you desire. Pillow, I say, shutting off the light and turning to address my steadfast headrest with respect, please wake me at six a.m.. I repeat my request politely three times, and pull the blanket up under my chin. Pillow, says my husband, the lark, please wake me at five forty-five.

○

Twilight of the Pillows. The Unbearable Lightness of Pillows. The Journey-Book of Excellence in Pillows. A Farewell to Pillows. On the Revolution of the Heavenly Pillows. The Scarlet Pillow. In Search of Lost Pillows. On the Origin of Pillows. Moby Pillow.

○

Someday I'll be a weather-beaten skull resting on a grass pillow, serenaded by a stray bird or two, wrote Ryokan. Kings and commoners end up the same, no more enduring than last night's dream.

○

If you want to go to sleep, kiss your pillow goodnight.

ACKNOWLEDGMENTS

Thanks to the editors at *BOMB*, *A Public Space*, *jubilat*, and *The Walrus*, where excerpts from this book first appeared. Thanks to the National Endowment for the Arts, the Canada Council for the Arts, and the Jeannette Haien Ballard Writers' Trust for their sustaining gifts. Thanks to the editors and staff at Canarium and House of Anansi for their enduring patience, commitment, and care. Thanks to the many generous friends whose conversations and questions about this work gave it shape. Thanks to my family for their love and support, and to Miosotis Guilfu for making the daily work of this possible. Thanks to Chicu for his hand in every draft. Thanks to Mira for her light.

Suzanne Buffam's first collection of poetry, *Past Imperfect*, was named a Book of the Year by the *Globe and Mail*. Her second collection, *The Irrationalist*, was a finalist for the Griffin Poetry Prize. She lives in Chicago.